LIFE RESUMED

After a Catastrophic Event or Other Loss

Paulina Rael Jaramillo, M.A.

Acknowledgements
Book cover design by: Michele Bryer and Ashlyn Bryer
Photography provided by: Kaitlyn Bryer

Scripture quotations are from The Holy Bible: New International Version,
New King James Version and English Standard Versions

Disclaimer: *Life Resumed: After a Catastrophic Event or Other Loss*, is written for the
sole purpose of providing inspiration, encouragement and hope and is not intended
to take the place of professional counseling.

www.Grief-Recovery.org

ISBN: 978-0-578-67874-0
PRJ Publishers

43266095R00291

Made in the USA
San Bernardino, CA
17 December 2016

What Readers Are Saying

Ms Jaramillo's newest book, *Life Resumed*...allows the reader to personalize their experience as they gain new insight and understanding into their own loss(es) and healing process. While quotes provided throughout the book are primarily Christian in nature they offer universal wisdom and spiritual reflection which is appropriate for all persons and beliefs. A helpful book for both individuals and grief support programs whether faith-based or not. —Victoria Stephan, The Stephan Center

This book could not have come to me at a more perfect time. I have recently experienced several great losses in my life, and I have found this book to be poignant, easy to read and a great comfort to me and my family. Ms. Paulina Jaramillo is a gifted writer and her book will comfort and inspire the lives of many. Kim Andreson, RN

Life Resumed is a wonderful faith based book that I found helpful, healing and enlightening. Paulina Jaramillo guides you through the steps to work through any kind of disruption...Death, divorce, or any other tragedy. I especially liked the thought provoking questions that you can write answers to in the book. I got a lot out of this book. It helped me learn to deal with my anger and hurt, (with the help of God) and begin to surrender and let go. I highly recommend *Life Resumed.* Cathy Pierro

Reading and working my way through *Life Resumed*...was like spending time with a wise and trusted friend who knew just what to say and more important what to ask - to heal the wounds and tame the ghosts that otherwise would deprive me of peace. I like that it is also part journal that can be revisited in the future. I'll be keeping *Life Resumed* close by for those times when life is disruptive again. Jack Flemmings

What Readers Are Saying (Page 2)

Covers a wide range of losses and provides a realistic approach to recovery. In reading *(Life Resumed)*, I approached it both as a clinician and as someone who has had many significant losses. I can see that it would be useful as a tool....with a therapist but it is also presented in such a way that anyone grieving any loss could read it and work independently toward recovery. I highly recommend *"Life Resumed"* —Judy Figal, MSW

In the face of loss whether it be by death of a loved one or some other tragedy, a person needs both emotional support and practical advice. Jaramillo provides both in *(Life Resumed)*. She speaks partly from her own experiences and partly from her educational background, so that she succeeds in bringing together the empathy and practicality one needs to get through times of loss. This is a book to read and to keep for future reference. —Randy Strickland, M.Div., M.S.

This book walks you through a journey of reflection and healing. Each page is carefully laid out with wonderful and encouraging words to help through difficult times. The author does a wonderful job outlining complications that one may experience through life's challenges and sharing various resources that are available to assist. This book is a great resource in itself, the author has a way of helping the reader to feel heard and understood. —Maggie Harris, MFT

Pertinent. Extremely helpful. Encourages hope/strength while promoting solutions if approached honestly & prayerfully. Wish I read *(Life Resumed)* sooner. Teddy R., RN

...I have set before you an open door,

which no one is able to shut.

I know that you have but little power,

and yet you have kept my word

and have not denied my name.

Revelation 3:8

This section is dedicated to

all who have lost loved ones

or have been adversely affected

in any way by COVID-19

or other catastrophic events.

Contents

(continued next page)

The Lord is good,

A stronghold in the day of trouble;

And He knows those who

trust in Him.

Nahum 1:7

Contents

Part 1:

Life Resumed

He has sent Me to heal the brokenhearted,

to proclaim liberty to the captives

and the opening of the prison

to those who are bound;

Isaiah 61:1

Efforts and courage
are not enough without
purpose and direction.

John F. Kennedy

Purpose and Intent

♦ Help you to name and own your behavior and emotions that are often present as a result of a catastrophic event or other loss.

♦ Help you to examine the source and nature of your feelings in order to release them.

♦ Help you to move forward by connecting to God, your own strength and enlisting help from other sources.

♦ Help you to let go of the past and connect with a richer and more fulfilling life in the present.

♦ Help you to discover your life's purpose and set new goals.

From the dawn of time,
God has known you and loved you.
He's not waiting today
for you to get it together.
He's waiting for you to come to Him
with open, empty hands.

-Dr. Bruce Wilkinson

Preparing to Write

Important

- Read and write on a daily basis
- Schedule an uninterrupted block of time
- Turn off all electronic devices
- Ask God for guidance and direction
- Write on the subject that's foremost in your mind
- Express your feelings without self criticism or editing

Not Important

- Spelling
- Grammar
- Content
- Penmanship

Look Up

Look Around

Look Beyond

Life After Lockdown

But those who hope in the Lord

will renew their strength.

They will soar on wings like eagles;

they will run and not grow weary,

they will walk and not be faint.

Isaiah 40:31

There is a sacredness in tears.
They are not the mark
of weakness, but of power.
They speak more eloquently
than ten thousand tongues.
They are messengers
of overwhelming grief...
and unspeakable love.

Washington Irving

Introduction

Tragedy and disasters create enormous disruption, anxiety and confusion. Not only has our normal routine been shattered—the aftermath of the catastrophe, whether it's a flood, a fire or a pandemic, needs to be controlled and redirected.

While all tragedies are challenging, recovering from a pandemic is especially daunting because we're experiencing loss from many sources and traveling through unfamiliar territory. Our physical health and the health of our loved ones has been at risk, our emotional well-being has been severely tested, and our relationships and income have been greatly impacted. And looming like a dark cloud is the question—how will I be able to cope if my life is radically altered?

Personal experience has taught me that we can chose to agonize over the answer to that question or we can choose to trust God's ability to reclaim and redeem the situation. One choice will keep us defeated, the other will enable us to move forward with greater strength and maturity.

Due to many factors, including our unique life experiences, all of us react to tragedy in a different way. Individual reactions are influenced by many factors including: personality, age, physical health, support system, state of mind at the time of the disaster, etc. Therefore, each person adjusts and works through the aftermath in their own way and at their own pace. Not everyone experiences the

I consider that our present sufferings

are not worth comparing

with the glory

that will be revealed in us.

Romans 8:18

same range of emotions nor experiences them to the same degree. Some individuals may feel depression more intensely than anger or perhaps worry becomes a greater issue.

Oftentimes a person may regress to a stage they had previously gone through and worry that they are not moving forward. Regression, however, is not a sign that healing is not taking place but rather that more work needs to be done at that stage. Given the uncertainty of life and the fact that we live in a changing and stressful world, something may occur in the present that creates a temporary set-back, causing negative emotions to surface. If that happens, pick-up where you left off and continue working through the stages at your own speed and in your own way. Recovery will take time and the final result may be different than expected.

Seeds of faith are always with us;
sometimes it takes a crisis to nourish
and encourage their growth.

-Susan L. Taylor

The Impact

Adjusting to a new way of life may not be what we want. However, attempting to live our lives in the past, would essentially mean living in denial (see pages 79-85). This would give rise to an entire cluster of new issues causing us to spiral downward into a sea of negative emotions and self-defeating behaviors.

Most of us are capable of making adjustments without too much effort, and some of us have gotten quite good at it due to the series of tragedies that have impacted our lives. However, dealing with the aftermath of a pandemic is something most of us have not experienced. As a result, we're facing a new experience and a new way of life which may include:

- *Working less hours*
- *Finding a new job*
- *Loss of income*
- *Health concerns for ourselves and others*
- *Loss of a loved one*
- *Delayed or cancelled events or celebrations*
- *Readjusting to socializing*

Our personal reaction to tragedy can range from extensive to mild, immediate to delayed, long-term to short-lived. Some days will be filled with forward movement, other days less so. There will even be days when we're ready to quit because we

Sometimes when we get overwhelmed

we forget how big God is.

A.W. Tozer

seem to be moving backward. However, depending on various factors, including our perspective and our trust in God, the outcome may have surprising and positive results. In my case, it opened up a new ministry and a new career path—helping others heal from catastrophic loss.

Below is a list of common reactions that most people experience after a tragic event.

Ways That Disasters Impact Your Life

- Stress, anxiety, fatigue, disorientation
- Depression, feeling overwhelmed, anger
- Shock, detachment
- Worry about the future
- Lonely, isolated, withdrawn
- Physically ill (Headaches, insomnia, eating disorders, weight loss/gain)
- Resentment, holding others responsible
- Alcohol or drug abuse
- Suicidal or self-harm tendencies
- Fear, paranoia

Set me free from my prison,

that I may praise your name...

Psalm 142:7

Regroup and Recover

Recovery is a process that takes time and requires commitment. While others may support and encourage us, the work is primarily our own. Taking action begins by acknowledging our feelings and vulnerability and seeking God's strength for the task. This is followed by a conscious decision to move forward and to continue forging ahead regardless of the set-backs and obstacles we may encounter.

I've found that writing my personal commitment down gives it greater validity and allows me to read it on a daily basis. I leave enough space at the bottom of the paper to add scripture verses or progress notes from time-to-time to help me stay focused and motivated (see example on page 75).

Look Up

Humbling ourselves and realizing that we can't do it alone, is probably the single most healing action that we can take. As humans we've been blessed with an array of abilities that enable us to make decisions, adjust our course and even fight to save our lives and/or the lives of others. Pride; however, is a negative state of mind that keeps us from asking and receiving the help we need at a time when we need it most. And even worse, pride puts us in a place of superiority toward God and destroys any possibility of an intimate relationship with Him.

God tries our faith

so that we may try His faithfulness.

Unknown

Years of struggle have taught me many lessons. The most important is the extent of God's patience and love as He waits for me to "Be still and know that I am God." (Psalm: 46:10 NKJV). After years of relying on my own strength to bring order out of chaos and peace out of turmoil, without much success, I've learned to release my pride and receive His grace.

The second lesson I learned is to seek Him first, while I'm still in the midst of my anguish, rather than seeking advice from others and eventually coming around to Him. God is trustworthy. He will never disclose our deepest secrets. He gives us strength when we're drained, brings clarity to our confusion and points us in the right direction.

In recent years, I've noticed a tendency for my prayers to increase as my stress levels mount. My prayers may be less than a minute or much longer in length, they may take place while I'm driving or working or upon waking up from a bad dream. And, depending upon the situation, my prayers might start out somewhat scattered and desperate but as I continue praying my mind becomes calmer and more focused until I'm able to view the situation from a different perspective.

Replying to the prompts on the following page will help you get started.

When life presents more challenges

than you can handle, delegate to God.

He not only has the answer, He is the answer.

-Travis Smiley

What am I facing that's beyond my ability to deal with?

_____
_____
_____
_____
_____
_____

How do I want God to help me? (*Be specific.*)

_____
_____
_____
_____
_____
_____

Has God helped me in the past?

_____
_____
_____
_____

If the above answer is yes. When? How? (*Include small and big instances.*)

_____
_____
_____
_____
_____
_____

Although the world is full of suffering,

it is also full of the overcoming of it.

Helen Keller

Reach Out

Although a certain amount of personal space is healthy, purposely isolating ourselves and blaming others for the tragedy is damaging to everyone involved. It will also compound the situation by adding more conflict and worst of all, will keep us locked in rather than moving forward. As human beings we're blessed with an enormous amount of resourcefulness and adaptability, but we were never meant to carry the entire load alone.

Sharing with others can help us regain perspective and their input may expose us to new and different solutions that we may not have considered otherwise. Another benefit to being open and vulnerable is what I call the *cleansing effect*. If done properly, it allows us to set our pride aside, get real with people and in so doing, live our lives with greater integrity and genuineness.

As you move toward healing make a determined effort to reach out to someone you trust (family, friends, coworkers, sibling, pastor, etc.) and let them know how you're feeling. This can be done over the phone, online or in person. Connecting and sharing with someone we trust reminds us that we're not alone and increases our faith and assurance that we will triumph over adversity.

Replying to the prompts on the following page will help you take action.

Reach boldly for the miracle.

God knows your gifts,

your hindrances,

and the condition you're in

at every moment.

-Dr. Bruce Wilkinson

Who can I trust with my confidences?

_____

_____

_____

_____

_____

What do I expect to gain by sharing?

_____

_____

_____

_____

_____

The areas I'll be open and vulnerable in are the following... (*Be specific.*)

_____

_____

_____

_____

_____

How will I show that I'm listening and considering their input? (*body language, asking questions if something isn't clear, etc.*)

_____

_____

_____

_____

_____

_____

Trust God in the dark till the light returns.

A.W. Tozer

Consider Counseling

Emotions can escalate quickly. Anger can turn into rage, sadness into depression, fear into paranoia and hopelessness into thoughts of suicide, especially if we feel alone and unsupported. In some cases, a situation that takes place in the present, such as a careless comment or perhaps a thoughtless reply made by someone we barely know, can become a trigger and cause us to overreact. Reactions that are out of proportion with the current situation usually stem from issues that haven't been dealt with and are still unresolved.

If that's happening to you with increasing regularity, you might consider scheduling one-on-one sessions with a therapist that's trained to assist with crisis recovery. Working through the tragedy with a professional you trust can help put the situation into perspective and provide a more balanced view. Therapy doesn't necessarily have to be long and drawn out, oftentimes as few as six sessions followed by a support group can make a huge difference.

Most health insurances have plans that allow a certain number of sessions with a small co-pay. Local counties also provide free or low-cost counseling sessions for qualifying individuals or families.

For a list of websites with additional information see page 41.

Release the need to know why

things happen as they do.

Instead, ask for the insight

to recognize what you're meant to learn.

-Carolyn Myss and Peter Occhlogrosso

What feelings am I experiencing that are beyond my ability to control?

_____

_____

_____

_____

_____

What kind of help do I expect to get from attending counseling sessions? (_Be specific._)

_____

_____

_____

_____

_____

_____

Who can I contact that will refer me to a therapist they trust? (_friends, primary caregiver, etc._)

_____

_____

_____

_____

_____

_____

Will my insurance cover the cost? Is there a copay?

_____

_____

_____

_____

Create in me a pure heart,

O God, and renew

a steadfast spirit within me.

Psalm 51:10

Resources

Mental Health, Treatment and Prevention Lifelines

www.samhsa.gov/esmi-treatment-locator

www.mentalhealth.gov/get-help/health-insurance

www.hhs.gov/programs/index.html

www.veteranscrisisline.net/

www.suicidepreventionlifeline.org/

www.healthunlocked.com/anxiety-depression-support?popup=1

www.moneyunder30.com/affordable-therapy

Watch,

stand fast in the faith,

be brave,

be strong.

Let all that you do

be done with love.

(1Corinthians 16:13-14 NKJV)

We can do no great things,

only small things with great love.

Mother Teresa

Make a Plan

After a catastrophic event, our lives are turned upside down due to the enormous disruption and confusion. Taking control by putting together a plan of action has a healing effect and helps us regain a feeling of normalcy. It gives us a sense of purpose and provides us with a goal to work toward.

First on the list should be the items we need to attend to right away. Items requiring our immediate attention may include: funeral or memorial service arrangements, finding a place to move into temporarily, contacting lawyers or insurances, reviewing our financial situation and discussing loan payments options with the bank. Meeting together as a family and writing the plan down will provide something tangible to refer to and serve as a reminder of your commitment. Be sure to allow space for any necessary adjustments that need to be made.

The outline I use is simple and easy to follow. First, I list the problem(s) on the left side of a blank piece of paper, followed by the hoped for solution in the second column and lastly, I write the actions I need to take to achieve the solution in the third column.

A word of caution, avoid making major life decisions during or immediately after a crisis. Switching career or jobs, making big purchases, ending or starting an intimate relationship and other life altering decisions are highly stressful in themselves and even harder to deal with when recovering from a disaster.

Use the prompts on the following page as a guideline to help you get started.

The key to happiness is realizing

that it's not what happens to you

that matters,

it's how you choose to respond.

-Keith D. Harrell

What arrangement(s) do I need to make immediately? (*If several, list in order of importance.*)

_____

_____

_____

_____

_____

_____

Who do I need to contact to make the arrangements?

_____

_____

_____

_____

_____

I plan to meet with family members on... *(date, time and place)*

_____

_____

_____

_____

Topics I would like us to address during our meeting are...

_____

_____

_____

_____

_____

_____

Wait on the Lord;

be of good courage

and He shall

strengthen your heart...

Psalm 27:14

Chill Out

Getting back to your previous routine may not be possible. Your life has been altered and will never be exactly the same as it was before. You may need to modify your routine by deleting and/or adding some things or better yet, establishing a new routine altogether. See this as an opportunity to expand and develop rather than an imposition.

Challenge yourself and encourage family members to eat healthy, well-balanced meals, exercise or spend time outdoors and get plenty of sleep. Make time to do things you enjoy as a family. Children especially need to be encouraged to try new foods and activities and the best way to help them is to model the behavior yourself. Start with small changes and add bigger and more challenging ones as they adjust. Be flexible, if something isn't working let it go and try something else. Make it fun and interesting.

If insomnia is an ongoing issue, you may be able to find relief through relaxation techniques such as: prayer, deep breathing, stretching, walking, exercising, etc. Avoid alcohol and drugs. They tend to have a numbing effect and can detract from and delay the healing process. Overuse of prescribed medication can also cause physical and/or emotional dependency and create problems rather than provide solutions.

For a list of websites with additional information see page 51.

Until today,

you may have been holding on to things

for fear they would not be replaced.

Just for today,

imagine what your life would be like

if you were to receive something better than

what you're holding on to right now.

-Iyanla Vanzant

Things that are important to include in our routine are... *(healthier food items, outings, hobbies, etc.)*

_____

_____

_____

_____

_____

How can I make our meals more nutritional? (*List items you can add or delete.)*

_____

_____

_____

_____

_____

What type of exercise/activities can we incorporate into our schedule? (*walks, bike riding, etc.*)

_____

_____

_____

_____

_____

What indoor activities can we do together? (*board games, charades, puzzles, etc.*)

_____

_____

_____

_____

_____

Prosperity is not in what you have attained

but rather in what you give away—

for it is only when you become empty

that you can be filled with something greater.

-Daniel Levin

We Are Not Alone

Considering the uniqueness of our personalities, the way we normally respond to problems and the roles that we assume in life, it's not surprising that healing is also a unique and individual process. Individual, in the sense that ultimately each one of us must find our own way regardless of the help and encouragement we receive from family and friends.

Catastrophes, whether an out-of-control virus or one that's weather related, tend to be cyclic. In all likelihood, we'll experience several in our lifetime. And due to their unpredictability, each one will affect us differently. Yet, in all of this, we're not completely alone--none of us would prevail if we were.

God, who is as near to us as our next breath, often sends help in unexpected ways: The job offer that comes at the right moment, the medical report that comes back negative or the car accident that was narrowly avoided. Blessings and protection come in all shapes and sizes. Our task is to remain open so that we can receive them.

Resources

Coping With Daily Life

www.cdc.gov/coronavirus/2019-ncov/daily-life-coping/index.html

www.sleepfoundation.org/insomnia/treatment/what-do-when-you-cant-sleep

www.umassmed.edu/globalassets/psychiatry/cbti/overcoming_ insomnia_ session_5.pdf

Earth hath no sorrow
that Heaven cannot heal.

Thomas Moore

Helping Your Children Recover

As adults we have a history of loss, grief and recovery. We often use information based on past experiences to make determinations about the present situation and use logic to help us remain calm and resolve problems. Whereas, children lack experience and tend to process stressful situations purely through their emotions which are often exaggerated.

Children pick up cues from the adults around them. If they hear words and see behavior that indicates hopelessness; they will act accordingly. If in turn, they're unable to express their emotions verbally or lack adequate support and encouragement, they may resort to negative behavior that can range from nightmares to outright rebellion and self-destructive behavior.

It's important to sit together and listen to their fears and doubts without being judgmental or downplaying their concerns. Due to their inability to express their emotions or inexperience in starting a conversation, we may need to help them. A good way to begin a dialog is by using open-ended questions such as, "you seem to be having a lot of nightmares. You've woken up screaming a few times this week. I would like to help you. Tell me what you're feeling."

It's also important to remind them of your love and commitment to protect them. And even more important, to reassure them that God is in control and will not only walk with them through the difficult times, He will ultimately bring good out of the tragedy. Praying together and reading scripture will demonstrate your own faith and trust in God.

If you worry about what might be,

and wonder what might have been,

you will ignore what is.

Author Unknown

According to the Centers for Disease Control (CDC), "Immediately after a disaster, children and adolescents have these common emotional behavioral reactions."

- Ages 1 to 5: Disobedience, fear of being separated from caregiver, and difficulty sleeping.

- Ages 6 to 10: Disobedience, fear of returning to school, and difficulty concentrating on tasks.

- Ages 11 to 18: Rebellious behavior, antisocial behavior and depression.

During and shortly after a disaster children and adolescent's fears are exceptionally high. It's very important that parents and caregivers give them extra attention and reassurance during and immediately following the event. Answering their questions truthfully without being vague or dismissive and in age appropriate terms, is also very important.

Some points to keep in mind are:

- Let them know (in age appropriate terms) how you're feeling about the situation and encourage them to share their feelings with you.

- Reassure them that you're available to answer their questions and help them with their fears.

- Reassure them that the situation will pass and talk about plans for the future. Encourage them to participate in the discussion.

- Establish a routine even if it's not exactly the same as the previous one. This provides structure and a sense of security.

Little faith will bring your soul to heaven,
but great faith will bring heaven
to your soul

Charles H. Spurgeon

Although a child will often develop Post Traumatic Stress Disorder (PTSD) after experiencing a traumatic event, some children do not. Various factors including their maturity, perspective, amount of support, etc. can have a positive influence.

According to The National Child Traumatic Stress Network, the following factors may also play a positive role in helping a child adjust without trauma.

Severity of the event. How serious was the event? How badly was the child or someone she loves physically hurt? Did they or someone they love need to go to the hospital? Were the police involved? Were children separated from their caregivers? Were they interviewed by a principal, police officer, or counselor? Did a friend or family member die?

Proximity to the event. Was the child actually at the place where the event occurred? Did they see the event happen to someone else or were they a victim? Did the child watch the event on television? Did they hear a loved one talk about what happened?

Caregivers' reactions. Did the child's family believe that he or she was telling the truth? Did caregivers take the child's reactions seriously? How did caregivers respond to the child's needs, and how did they cope with the event themselves?

Prior history of trauma. Children continually exposed to traumatic events are more likely to develop traumatic stress reactions.

Feed your faith,

and your doubts

will starve to death.

Our Daily Bread

Family and community factors. The culture, race, and ethnicity of children, their families, and their communities can be a protective factor, meaning that children and families have qualities and or resources that help buffer against the harmful effects of traumatic experiences and their aftermath. One of these protective factors can be the child's cultural identity. Culture often has a positive impact on how children, their families, and their communities respond, recover, and heal from a traumatic experience. However, experiences of racism and discrimination can increase a child's risk for traumatic stress symptoms.

If your child or adolescent's behavior is causing problems or creating disruption for himself or others you might consider starting a conversation with them to discuss the issue (see page 61). Focus on the behavior that's causing the most difficulty (i.e. yelling and hitting). Resist bringing up several problems at any one time. Ignoring negative behavior in the hopes that it goes away never works. Eventually, suppressed emotions can lead to self-defeating and/or self-destructive behavior. Talking and listening without making assumptions or judgments will bring the issue out in the open and may avert more severe consequences.

Make others the focal point.

Give generously, listen intently,

praise freely and love unceasingly.

-Travis Smiley

The MentalHealth.gov website provides the following guidelines for initiating conversation.

How to Talk About Mental Health

- Can you tell me more about what is happening?
- How you are feeling?
- Have you had feelings like this in the past?
- Sometimes you need to talk to an adult about your feelings. I'm here to listen. How can I help you feel better?
- Do you feel like you want to talk to someone else about your problem?
- I'm worried about your safety. Can you tell me if you have thoughts about harming yourself or others?

If your child's negative behavior persists or escalates over time, you might want to consider professional help. Some families prefer to start with their church pastor or school counselor. Other options include state and local governments which offer many different types of programs for families and children of all ages (see page 63).

The Wellness Recovery Action Plan (WRAP) is intended to be used in a peer-support group context and is appropriate for people of all ages. The Psychological First Aid (PFA) and Skills for Psychological Recovery (SPR) were developed by the National Center for PTSD and the National Child Traumatic Stress Network, to assist in disaster response and recovery.

God sleeps through storms

and calms the winds with a word...

He was here before they came.

He'll be here after they're gone.

–Max Lucado

Below is a list of websites that provide additional information.

www.samhsa.gov/programs

www.nctsn.org/treatments-and-practices/psychological-first-aid-and-skills-for-psychological-recovery

www.cdc.gov/childrensmentalhealth/index.html

www.cdc.gov/coronavirus/2019-ncov/daily-life-coping/children.html

www.ready.gov/kids

www.nctsn.org/what-is-child-trauma/about-child-trauma

www.mentalhealth.gov/talk

From the beginning of time to the present and well into the future, communities and families exist and thrive as a result of cooperation and commitment to one another and their faith in God.

Parents and caregivers are in a unique position to help their children and each other. The connection that already exists among family members and the natural desire that parents have for their children's well-being, provides the ideal place for healing and nurturing to flourish.

Encouraging children be hopeful and to put their trust in God is a good starting point. However, simply telling them without modeling the behavior we're asking them to acquire is hypocritical. We need to demonstrate patience, understanding, kindness, forgiveness, etc., toward them and one another in order for our words to carry meaning and our role as parents to be effective.

A better world shall emerge

based on faith and understanding.

-Douglas MacArthur

Could It Happen Again?

All of us want reassurance that another pandemic or catastrophic event won't happen or at least not in our lifetime. But even as I sit here writing, I feel the tremors of an earthquake shaking the ground in my home state of California. Although the quake was small by usual standards (4.9 on the Richter Scale), it still caused me to bemoan, "Not an earthquake on top of everything else."

I continued typing while sitting on the edge of my chair ready to duck under my desk if the tremors worsened. I imagined the added havoc and chaos a large earthquake would create. How would we help each other during lockdown? How would the already overburdened medical profession cope? How would... Then I remembered Job. The biblical prophet who in rapid succession lost everything that he'd spent a lifetime acquiring (business, income, children, health). What impresses me most about him, is his calm response to the desperate confrontation from his wife as he sat on a heap of ashes scraping the boils on his skin with a piece of broken clay. "Shall we indeed accept good from God, and shall we not accept adversity?" (Job 2:10 NKJV)

Although my personal suffering doesn't compare with Job's suffering, I've learned that God allows adversity for a purpose and within the adversity He embeds many lessons. Our task is to learn them.

There is no ironclad promise that we won't be struck down again, but there is reassurance. Because the One who knows all things and controls all things, has given us His solemn vow of protection, "When you pass through the waters, I will be with you; and through the rivers, they shall not overwhelm you; when you walk through fire you shall not be burned..." (Isaiah 43:2 ESV).

Life After Loss

Everyone grieves when someone dies,

but if we are to heal,

we must also mourn.

Alan Wolfelt, PhD

Be in control of my life Lord,

and give me peace

in knowing that You are.

Paulina Jaramillo

This Section
is Dedicated To
And
In Loving Memory Of:

Selina Jaramillo

Eugenia Rael Rodriquez

Eugenio Rodriguez

Frank Bonilla

Raymond Jaramillo Trujillo

Robert Jaramillo Trujillo

Patrick Jaramillo

Charley Garcia

Wilma Jaramillo

George Jaramillo

Olivia Jaramillo Garcia

Grief has a beginning,

but it also has an end.

H. Norman Wright

Losses and Conditions that Cause Grieving

* Death
* Divorce
* Chronic Illness
* Personal Injury
* Miscarriage
* Marital Separation
* Epidemic/Pandemic
* Natural Disaster
* Civil Unrest and violence
* Relationship Break-up
* Job Reassignment
* Job Demotion
* Unemployment
* Financial Loss
* Foreclosure
* Pet Loss
* Retirement
* Relocation
* Imprisonment
* Empty-nest Syndrome
* Altered Working Conditions
* Altered Living Conditions
* Revision of Personal Habits
* Loss of: Trust, Approval, Safety
* Change in Social Status
* Unfulfilled Life Goals

Faith is taking the first step

even when you don't

see the whole staircase.

Martin Luther King, Jr.

Introduction

Healing after the death of a loved one, a divorce, or any life altering situation is a deeply personal experience and by its very nature—a lonely process. Grieving involves the sentiments and emotions connected to loss. Mourning is the expression of those feelings. In order for healing to take place, you must acknowledge your loss and give yourself permission to mourn as you seek God's abundant mercy and healing grace.

Due to the uniqueness of your loss, your life experiences and your emotional connection to what's been lost, you'll experience grief in a way that's unique to you. However, most people experience many of the same emotions at one time or another, with depression being the most common (see pages 141-149).

It's important to remember that healing is a gradual process. It can't be hurried nor accomplished in a predetermined length of time. In fact, emotions that you thought you had dealt with may reappear at a later date. But even those moments of regression are evidence that healing is taking place and serve as signals that more work needs to be done at that particular stage.

Like all journeys, healing begins with a single step, followed by a second and a third, until the destination is finally reached and the peace that you long for is yours. As you begin to heal and release your attachment to a person or lifestyle that's no longer a part of your life, you'll open yourself to new possibilities. Eventually, the memories that are now painful will become memories that you can cherish and treasure.

Life is a wilderness
of twists and turns
where faith is
your only compass.

Paul Santaguida

<u>My Journey Toward Healing Commitment</u>

Get started on your journey toward healing by reading and agreeing to the paragraph below and by replying to the prompts on page 77.

I, _____, (*your name*) am eager to reclaim my life and live it more abundantly. I realize that healing requires time, energy and commitment. Therefore, I commit to working faithfully and prayerfully on a daily basis. I will be as open and honest as I can be so that my healing can begin and progress without hindrance. I will overcome any obstacles that would prevent me from working and progressing on my journey toward healing. I will celebrate each accomplishment that I make and will remain open to and receive the restoration that God has for me.

There isn't a person anywhere
who isn't capable of doing more
than he thinks he can.

Henry Ford

My favorite quiet spot is…

_____
_____
_____
_____
_____
_____
_____
_____
_____

My prayer/desire for guidance and healing is…

_____
_____
_____
_____
_____
_____
_____
_____
_____

Scriptures and quotations that encourage me are…

_____
_____
_____
_____
_____
_____
_____
_____
_____

Send forth your light and your truth,

let them guide me;

let them bring me to your holy mountain,

to the place where you dwell.

Psalm 43:3

Beyond Denial

Denial serves a purpose—at least in the beginning. It helps to cushion the initial shock and enables you to make whatever arrangements need to be made. But when denial is used to avoid reality it becomes a cushion with a false bottom.

When tragedy strikes, denial can seem like a way to escape the unbearable and overwhelming reality. However, stifling emotions connected to loss creates additional complications for the simple reason that suppressed emotions don't stay suppressed. Sooner or later they'll begin to surface with greater-than-ever intensity, oftentimes causing you to behave in a way that's not in keeping with your usual lifestyle such as: risk-taking, gambling, chemical abuse, etc. Unresolved issues can also manifest themselves through clinical depression and/or chronic illness.

Dealing with emotions means facing reality and that in turn means grappling with all the feelings that you're experiencing. Thankfully, not all of them have to be dealt with at once. You can examine and work through them as they emerge. While dealing with raw emotions may not sound very appealing—living your life fully and with purpose is worth the effort it will take to reach that goal.

The following pages are designed to help you work through any denial that you may be experiencing.

The Serenity Prayer

God grant me the serenity

to accept the things I cannot change;

courage to change the things I can;

and wisdom to know the difference.

Reinhold Niebuhr

What occurred recently that caused dramatic changes in my life?

_____
_____
_____
_____
_____
_____
_____
_____
_____

How have those changes impacted my life?

_____
_____
_____
_____
_____
_____
_____
_____
_____

I find it difficult to understand why…

_____
_____
_____
_____
_____
_____
_____
_____
_____

Life is eternal

and love is immortal;

And death is only a horizon,

And a horizon is nothing

save the limit of our sight.

Rossiter W. Raymond

I find it difficult to listen to…

_____
_____
_____
_____
_____
_____
_____

Because…

_____
_____
_____
_____
_____
_____
_____

I find it difficult to discuss…

_____
_____
_____
_____
_____
_____

Because…

_____
_____
_____
_____
_____
_____

Understanding can overcome any situation,

however mysterious or insurmountable

it may appear to be.

Norman Vincent Peale

What can I ask for that others don't know I need?

_____
_____
_____
_____
_____
_____
_____
_____
_____
_____
_____
_____
_____

Who can I ask? (*Trust is important.*)

_____
_____
_____
_____
_____
_____
_____
_____
_____
_____
_____
_____
_____

...weeping may remain for a night,

but rejoicing comes in the morning.

Psalm 30:5

Feel the Feeling

Feelings are a natural part of your emotional being and play a vital role in your life. Without feelings (and your reactions to them) life would be drab and colorless, and in some cases you could be in real danger. Emotions enable you to laugh when you hear a joke, empathize with the misfortune of another, react with anger when you see an injustice. They also serve to warn you of impending danger or when a situation is not safe. Feelings are illusive and transitory. They're also very real and can dictate how you live your life. Your goal is to admit and experience your emotions but not let them control who you are, what you do, or what you say.

The first step in working through your feelings begins with acknowledging that you're responsible for what you feel at any given moment. Although it's easier to assign responsibility to someone or something other than yourself, doing so causes you to revert back into denial.

Emotions are connected to expectations and perceptions. If you change how you perceive a situation, or what you expect from it, your emotions connected to that situation will change as well. Expressing your feelings verbally or in writing gives them meaning and clarity. It also helps you to acknowledge and release them and redirect their power in a more positive direction.

The following pages are designed to help you acknowledge and examine your emotions.

The walls we build around us

to keep sadness out

also keeps out joy.

Jim Rohn

Who is responsible for my feelings? Am I holding others accountable?

_____
_____
_____
_____
_____
_____
_____
_____
_____
_____
_____
_____
_____

What am I feeling right now?

_____
_____
_____
_____
_____
_____
_____
_____
_____
_____
_____
_____
_____
_____
_____

How precious to me

are your thoughts, O God!

How vast is the sum of them!

Were I to count them,

they would outnumber the grains of sand.

When I awake, I am still with you.

Psalm 139:17-18

If my feelings had color, what color would they be? *(Assign a different color to each one.)*

_____

_____

_____

_____

_____

_____

_____

_____

_____

_____

_____

_____

_____

What texture would they be? *(Assign a different texture to each one.)*

_____

_____

_____

_____

_____

_____

_____

_____

_____

_____

_____

_____

_____

Change your thoughts
and you change your world.

Norman Vincent Peale

What sound would they make? (*Assign a different sound to each one.*)

_____

_____

_____

_____

_____

_____

_____

_____

_____

_____

_____

_____

_____

_____

What would they taste like? (*Assign a different taste to each one.*)

_____

_____

_____

_____

_____

_____

_____

_____

_____

_____

_____

_____

_____

_____

Before you lash out in fear,

look up in faith.

Max Lucado

Feelings that I would like to share with others are…

_____

_____

_____

_____

_____

_____

_____

_____

Feelings that I'm reluctant to share are…

_____

_____

_____

_____

_____

_____

_____

_____

I'm reluctant to share those feelings because…

_____

_____

_____

_____

_____

_____

_____

_____

No one ever told me

that grief felt so like fear.

C.S. Lewis

Conquering Fear

Some people choose to isolate themselves rather than face their fears, not realizing that fear is a powerful emotion that can disguise itself in a variety of forms including anger and depression.

Losing someone or something (oftentimes abruptly) that you value can cause fear and anxiety. Your loss can bring about several changes which can include your identity and financial status. In addition to that is the fear of what lies ahead and the overwhelming feeling that you won't be able to cope. And lurking just around the corner is the fear of who or what you're going to lose next. Even the act of grieving is scary because of its intensity and unfamiliarity.

While healthy fear can serve to warn you of impending danger and enable you to take appropriate action, unhealthy fear can paralyze you or cause you to react in such a way as to create danger to yourself and/or others. The best way, and perhaps the only way, to conquer fear is by doing the very thing you fear most—facing it and dealing with it. Fortunately, you don't have to do it all at once. Conquering even one small fear will make you less afraid and more confident in your ability to free yourself from its grip.

The following pages are designed to help you face your fears and enable you to release them.

...do not fear, for I am with you;

do not be dismayed, for I am your God.

I will strengthen you and help you;

I will uphold you

with my righteous right hand.

Isaiah 41:10

What am I most afraid of?

_____

_____

_____

_____

_____

_____

_____

_____

_____

_____

_____

_____

What is the worst thing that can happen?

_____

_____

_____

_____

_____

_____

_____

_____

_____

_____

_____

Fear forces-Love leads,

Faith follows.

Keith Moore

How likely is it that my greatest fear(s) will come true?

_____
_____
_____
_____
_____
_____
_____
_____
_____
_____
_____
_____

Things that I do or say when I'm afraid are...

_____
_____
_____
_____
_____
_____
_____
_____
_____
_____
_____
_____
_____

For God has not given us

a spirit of fear

but of power and of love

and of a sound mind.

2 Timothy 1:7

Which of my fears are directly connected to and exaggerated by my recent loss(es)?

_____

_____

_____

_____

_____

_____

_____

_____

_____

_____

_____

How has fear affected my life? *(relationships, job performance, church or social involvement, etc.)*

_____

_____

_____

_____

_____

_____

_____

_____

_____

_____

_____

_____

We gain strength,

and courage and confidence

by each experience

in which we really stop

to look fear in the face...

Eleanor Roosevelt

If I was not afraid my life would improve in the following ways...

_____

_____

_____

_____

_____

_____

_____

_____

_____

What can I do to lessen my fear(s)?

_____

_____

_____

_____

_____

_____

_____

_____

My support group includes...*(family, friends, pastors, counselors, etc.)*

1. _____

2. _____

3. _____

4. _____

5. _____

6. _____

Don't hold on to anger, hurt or pain.

They steal your energy

and keep you from love.

Leo Buscaglia

Defusing Anger

Anger is a normal response to an unjust situation and, if directed properly, can serve to bring about positive change. However, anger can also be a reaction stemming from other emotions that have been suppressed (fear, guilt, hurt, etc.) Unfortunately, suppressed emotions are self-defeating and often lead to self-destructive behaviors which can include: anger rages, physical illness, chemical abuse, risk-taking, eating disorders, panic attacks, etc.

A telltale sign that anger is directly linked to suppressed emotions is the intensity and duration. If the reaction to a given situation is out of proportion to what occurred, you can be sure that other emotions are involved.

Anger can also be misdirected. When a tragedy or crisis occurs, you might be tempted to blame the doctor, the hospital, God, or anyone else that you feel could have averted the tragedy or was responsible for creating the crisis. Feelings of anger can also extend to others around you who have not suffered a loss and whose lives are seemingly calm and undisturbed. Admitting and working through your feelings of anger will help you to understand, diffuse and redirect the energy that suppressed emotions are stealing from you.

The following pages are designed to help you examine and express your feelings of anger constructively.

A wise man's heart

guides his mouth,

and his lips promote instruction.

Proverbs 16:23

I feel angry when…

_____

_____

_____

_____

_____

_____

_____

_____

_____

_____

_____

_____

I do or say the following when I feel angry…

_____

_____

_____

_____

_____

_____

_____

_____

_____

_____

_____

_____

_____

_____

Anger makes you smaller,

while forgiveness forces you

to grow beyond what you were.

Cherie Carter-Scott

Other people react to my anger by...

_____

_____

_____

_____

_____

_____

_____

_____

_____

_____

_____

_____

What other emotions are present just before or during an episode of anger *(fear, hurt, guilt, etc.)*?

_____

_____

_____

_____

_____

_____

_____

_____

_____

_____

_____

_____

Search me, O God,

and know my heart;

test me and know

my anxious thoughts.

See if there is any

offensive way in me,

and lead me

in the way everlasting.

Psalm 139:23-24

What's my anger telling me? *(See secondary emotions on the previous page.)*

_____

_____

_____

_____

_____

_____

_____

_____

_____

_____

_____

_____

_____

What personal change(s) do I need to make? *(perspective, attitude, etc.)*

_____

_____

_____

_____

_____

_____

_____

_____

_____

_____

_____

_____

_____

_____

_____

Let us not look back in anger

or forward in fear,

but around in awareness.

James Thurber

What *other* change(s) do I need to make? *(relationships, associations, activities, etc.)*

_____

_____

_____

_____

_____

_____

_____

_____

How/where can I express my anger constructively? *(prayer, counseling, support group, journaling, etc.)*

_____

_____

_____

_____

_____

_____

_____

_____

How would my life improve if I expressed my anger constructively?

_____

_____

_____

_____

_____

_____

_____

_____

He heals the brokenhearted
and binds up their wounds.

Psalm 147:3

Expressing Hurt

When a crisis or catastrophic event occurs, it's normal and even healthy to feel hurt. Some of the ways that hurt expresses itself is through feelings of sadness, disillusionment, depression and anger. These feelings can become intense, and when suppressed, can find an outlet through bouts of rage followed by guilt and self-loathing. When someone or something important to you has been lost, it's not unusual to experience feelings of abandonment or in the case of job loss, feelings of betrayal and despair. The pain is compounded by the chaos and profound impact it creates in your life.

In some cases, existing relationships may undergo transition or cease to exist altogether, which may add to the initial pain. People occasionally distance themselves from someone who's hurting because they don't know how to help, or in some cases, may be unable to as a result of their own issues.

Recognizing your hurt feelings and taking responsibility for your actions is an important step toward healing. In some cases you may wish to set new boundaries or evaluate existing relationships to determine if they're part of the problem.

The following pages will help you examine and release your feelings of hurt and make changes that may be necessary.

Sing like no one's listening,

love like you've never been hurt,

dance like nobody's watching,

and live like it's heaven on earth.

Mark Twain

I feel hurt when…

_____

_____

_____

_____

_____

_____

_____

_____

_____

_____

_____

_____

Are there people or situations in my life that are closely associated with those feelings? Who? What?

_____

_____

_____

_____

_____

_____

_____

_____

_____

_____

_____

_____

Let us then approach the throne

of grace with confidence,

so that we may receive

mercy and find grace

to help us in our time of need.

Hebrews 4:16

I usually do and/or say the following when I feel hurt...

_____

_____

_____

_____

_____

_____

_____

_____

_____

_____

_____

_____

Other people react to my expressions of hurt by...

_____

_____

_____

_____

_____

_____

_____

_____

_____

_____

_____

_____

_____

God will do wonders

with a broken heart

if you will give Him the pieces.

Unknown

Do my words, attitude and behavior hurt others? If so, which ones cause the most problems? Why?

_____

_____

_____

_____

_____

_____

_____

_____

_____

_____

_____

_____

_____

What do I need to do before I approach someone who has said or done something hurtful to me? *(evaluate my motive, pray for guidance, etc.)*

_____

_____

_____

_____

_____

_____

_____

_____

_____

_____

_____

_____

_____

For he has not despised or disdained

the suffering of the afflicted one;

he has not hidden his face from him

but has listened to his cry for help.

Psalm 22:24

If that person is not willing to listen or acknowledge my feelings I will…

_____

_____

_____

_____

_____

_____

_____

_____

Constructive ways that I would like to express my hurt feelings are…

_____

_____

_____

_____

_____

_____

_____

_____

_____

What changes do I need to make in my life? *(Evaluate existing relation-ships, set boundaries, seek counseling, etc.).*

_____

_____

_____

_____

_____

_____

_____

_____

The bitterest tears shed over graves

are for words left unsaid

and deeds left undone.

Harriet Beecher Stowe

Releasing Guilt

Unhealthy guilt is like a small sore that keeps getting bigger and causing more pain until it's so large that it affects the entire body. Wounds need to be attended to long before this happens.

Relationships are subject to the stress and strain of everyday life. There are times when you'll say or do something that you wish you hadn't, or perhaps fail to say or do something that you wish you had. When this happens and the person is no longer in your life, your thoughts can become distorted with feelings of guilt and remorse.

An important step in releasing unwanted shame and guilt is to write down in detail whatever obsessive thoughts and memories you're having. Be honest and straightforward. (The list will be discarded later.) The next step requires that you substitute negative thoughts with positive ones. On a separate sheet of paper write scripture that speaks of God's forgiveness and mercy. Two of my favorites verses are: "If we confess our sins, He is faithful and just to forgive us our sins and to cleanse us from all unrighteousness" (1 John 1:9 NKJV); and, "For you, Lord, are good and ready to forgive and abundant in mercy to all who call upon you." (Psalm 86:5 NKJV).

Lastly, seek God in prayer asking for forgiveness and healing then tear or shred the list containing your thoughts and memories. If/when they return, remind your-

Let go of old guilt

and remember that you're

God's perfect child.

-Doreen Virtue, Ph.D.

self that you've released them, repeat the scripture verse(s) and say a prayer. This process may have to be repeated several times before you experience freedom but each time that you repeat the procedure you'll be that much closer to your goal.

The following pages are designed to help you take a closer look at your thoughts and memories to determine if any of them are associated with guilt and guide you in releasing them.

We cannot change the past,

but we can change our attitude toward it.

Uproot guilt and plant forgiveness.

Tear out arrogance and seed humility.

Exchange love for hate;

thereby, making the present comfortable

and the future promising.

Maya Angelou

Persistent thoughts or memories that I'm having are…

_____

_____

_____

_____

_____

_____

_____

_____

_____

_____

_____

_____

Are they associated with something I said or did? *(Be specific.)*

_____

_____

_____

_____

_____

_____

_____

_____

_____

_____

_____

_____

_____

Each life is made up of

mistakes and learning,

waiting and growing,

practicing patience

and being persistent.

Billy Graham

Are they associated with something I wish I had said or done?
(Be specific.)

_____

_____

_____

_____

_____

_____

_____

_____

_____

_____

_____

_____

What types of feelings do they evoke? *(anger, fear, sadness, hurt, guilt, etc.)*

_____

_____

_____

_____

_____

_____

_____

_____

_____

_____

_____

_____

_____

Many of us crucify ourselves

between two thieves—

regret for the past

and fear of the future.

Fulton Oursler

When I feel guilty I do or say…

_____
_____
_____
_____
_____
_____
_____
_____

How is guilt affecting my life? *(physically, spiritually, mentally, emotionally)*

_____
_____
_____
_____
_____
_____
_____
_____
_____

If I didn't feel guilty my life would improve in the following ways…

_____
_____
_____
_____
_____
_____
_____
_____

And the peace of God

Which transcends all understanding

will guard your hearts and your minds

in Christ Jesus.

Philippians 4:7

Who can I share these thoughts or memories with? (*God, pastor, trusted friend, counselor, etc.*)

_____

_____

_____

_____

_____

_____

_____

_____

_____

_____

_____

_____

What else can I do to release them? (*write them down, pray, forgive myself and/or others, etc.*)

_____

_____

_____

_____

_____

_____

_____

_____

_____

_____

_____

_____

Forgiving does not erase the bitter past.

A healed memory

is not a deleted memory.

Instead, forgiving what we cannot forget

creates a new way to remember.

Lewis B. Smedes

Write three sentences that begin with: *"I forgive myself for…"*

1._____

_____

_____

_____

2._____

_____

_____

_____

3._____

_____

_____

_____

Write three sentences that begin with: *"I forgive _____ for…"*

1._____

_____

_____

_____

2._____

_____

_____

_____

3._____

_____

_____

God cannot give us

happiness and peace

apart from Himself,

because it is not there.

C. S. Lewis

Defeating Depression

Depression is an indication that something is wrong and needs your attention. Episodes of depression can be debilitating and insidious. They can affect your sleep, your appetite, the way you see yourself and your attitude toward life in general. Depression can create disruption in your professional life and lead to poor performance. It can also impact your personal relationships with family and friends, which in turn can increase feelings of depression.

Depression due to a crisis or a traumatic event is referred to as situational depression and is a normal reaction to loss. However, if left untreated, situational depression can lead to a more serious form referred to as clinical depression, especially in individuals with high risk factors.

Some of the symptoms of clinical depression include feelings of hopelessness, deep despair and suicidal tendencies (see page 223). If you're experiencing these symptoms get medical attention and consider counseling therapy. If seeing a therapist is not an option, consider sharing your feelings with a pastor or a trusted friend.

The following pages are designed to help you explore your feelings of depression and ways of overcoming them.

Though he fall,

he shall not be utterly cast down;

for the Lord upholds him

with His hand.

Psalm 37:24

I feel sad and/or depressed when…

_____
_____
_____
_____
_____
_____
_____
_____

I usually do the following when I feel sad and/or depressed…

_____
_____
_____
_____
_____
_____
_____
_____
_____

Others react to my feelings of depression by…

_____
_____
_____
_____
_____
_____
_____

Seasons of the Soul

Why am I cast down

And despondently sad

When I long to be happy

And joyous and glad?

Why is my heart heavy

With unfathomable weight

As I try to escape

This soul-saddened state?

I ask myself often,

What makes life this way.

Why is the song silenced

In the heart that was gay?

And then, with God's help

It all becomes clear...

And, Oh! What a blessing

To know there are reasons,

And to find that our soul

Must, too, have its seasons...

Helen Steiner Rice

Depression has affected my life in the following ways...

_____
_____
_____
_____
_____
_____
_____
_____
_____
_____
_____
_____
_____

Sometimes I feel so depressed that I find it difficult to... *(sleep, eat, work, smile, etc.)*

_____
_____
_____
_____
_____
_____
_____
_____
_____
_____
_____
_____

A bruised reed he will not break,

and a smoldering wick

he will not snuff out.

In faithfulness

he will bring forth justice...

Isaiah 42:3

What changes can I make in me or in my environment? *(pray for guidance, seek counseling, join a support group, volunteer)*

_____

_____

_____

_____

_____

_____

_____

Do I need to change my activity level, eating habits, sleep patterns? If yes, which ones?

_____

_____

_____

_____

_____

_____

_____

_____

How can I make those changes? *(Be specific.)*

_____

_____

_____

_____

_____

_____

_____

_____

_____

In the midst of winter,

I finally learned that there was in me

an invincible summer.

Albert Camus

Feelings and thoughts I would like to share with others are...

_____
_____
_____
_____
_____
_____
_____
_____
_____
_____
_____
_____
_____
_____
_____

Who can I share them with? *(Trust is important.)*

_____
_____
_____
_____
_____
_____
_____
_____
_____
_____
_____
_____
_____

There are things that we don't want
to happen but have to accept,
things we don't want to know
but have to learn,
and people we can't live without
but have to let go.

Author Unknown

Letting Go

I want to take a moment to congratulate you for the courage, strength and commitment that you've shown in working through the various stages on your journey toward healing. Each stage has been a stepping stone that's moved you farther along the path of wellness. Now it's time to let go of the past, reclaim your life and begin to live it in the abundance that God has for you.

Some of you may find this section and the following one (Saying Farewell) to be the most difficult, but also the most liberating. The reasons for the difficulty are complicated and multifaceted. Simply put, you're not only letting go of the person or situation, but of the lifestyle connected to them and/or the expectations that were not fulfilled. The future that "might have been" needs to be replaced with a new reality. Another cause of anxiety is the erroneous belief that letting go means forgetting the person. In reality, letting go means releasing the pain associated with your loss and opening yourself to embrace and cherish the memories that you made together.

Letting go is a process that requires faith and commitment. It also requires time and energy. Some of the stages may have to be repeated more than once before you experience healing. *But it will happen! God is faithful!*

Pages 153—157 are designed to help you examine your feelings in order to move forward.

When you surrender

and let go of the past,

you allow yourself

to be fully alive in the moment.

-Miguel Ruiz

Letting go is...

Trusting: God to provide strength and guidance.

Releasing: The person or situation because I choose to do so.

Appreciating: The time I was given with that person or in that situation.

Remembering: The person or situation for the positive influence they had in my life.

Recognizing: That life is full of new beginnings.

Seeking: New direction for my life.

Fulfilling: The purpose for which I was created.

God didn't promise days

without pain,

laughter without sorrow,

sun without rain,

but He did promise strength

for the day,

comfort for the tears

and light for the way.

Helen Steiner Rice

Letting go is difficult for me because....

_____
_____
_____
_____
_____
_____
_____
_____
_____
_____
_____
_____
_____
_____

Even though it's difficult, I choose to let go because...

_____
_____
_____
_____
_____
_____
_____
_____
_____
_____
_____
_____
_____
_____

Do not sorrow,

for the joy of the Lord

is your strength.

Nehemiah 8:10

What do I miss most about *(person or situation)* _____?

_____
_____
_____
_____
_____
_____
_____
_____
_____
_____
_____
_____

Expectations that will **not** be fulfilled with that person or in that situation are...

_____
_____
_____
_____
_____
_____
_____
_____
_____
_____
_____
_____
_____

Trust in the Lord

with all your heart

and lean not on your own understanding;

in all your ways

acknowledge Him,

and He will make your paths straight.

Proverbs 3:5-6

My fondest memory with that person or in that situation is...

_____

_____

_____

_____

_____

_____

_____

_____

_____

_____

_____

_____

_____

Memories that others have shared with me are...

_____

_____

_____

_____

_____

_____

_____

_____

_____

_____

_____

_____

_____

_____

_____

Nature's first green is gold,

Her hardest hue to hold.

Her early leaf's a flower,

But only so an hour.

Then leaf subsides to leaf.

So Eden sank to grief,

So dawn goes down to day.

Nothing gold can stay.

Robert Frost

A Final Farewell

I'd like to share with you my personal experience in letting go. Mom's death was the second in a series of 11 losses in our extended family (three of them within a 10-month period)! I was fortunate to be by Mom's bedside during her last moments. My voice and arms were the last earthly contact she had before receiving her spiritual body and entering into God's presence. Although I didn't hear divine music or see angelic beings, I nevertheless felt the power of God sustaining me. I've written a story about the experience titled "Life is for Living" and posted it on my website: www.Grief-Recovery.org.

Praying, hiking, reading, and journaling became a way for me to deal with the emotional accumulation of tragedies and their impact. Two years, a hundred miles and several journals later—when I could breathe again—I made a list of the various stages of grieving that I had experienced and what had been most helpful. That was the birth of my book set, *A Time To Heal: Grief Recovery Guide and Workbook* which I later combined and expanded into a single edition, *Life Interrupted: Grief Recovery Guide and Workbook*. It is my heartfelt desire that those books and the one your holding (*Life Resumed: After a Catastrophic Event or Other Loss*) will find their way into the hearts and lives of people who need healing and restoration and in some small way provide strength and hope.

The following exercise (pages 163-167) is designed to help you sort through your thoughts and feelings in the form of a farewell letter.

The peace we seek to win

is not victory over any other people,

but the peace that comes

with healing in its wings...

Richard M. Nixon

Do the following exercise in a private and quiet place.

Use the next two pages to write down your thoughts and feelings that you would like to include in a farewell letter. Write the final draft of your letter on a separate sheet of paper. This is your opportunity to say and ask all the things you wish you had but, for one reason or another, did not. If your loss involves a person due to death, divorce or a breakup, look at their picture while writing. If your loss is due to a life-altering crisis such as: unemployment, physical disability, chronic illness, etc., address your letter to the loss you're experiencing and/or the person(s) or circumstance(s) that you feel were responsible. Include anything that comes to your mind. It can be positive or negative as well as questions or answers. Don't censor your words. Instead, allow yourself to be straightforward and real, honest and open. When your letter is finished read it out loud and say a prayer of release. The next step in the letting go process is to shred or tear the letter.

Because nothing in life is quick and easy, you'll probably experience a resurgence of emotions from time to time as you continue to heal. If/when that happens, remind yourself that you've made a decision to embrace life, heal and move forward. If necessary, re-read "My Journey Toward Healing Commitment" on page 75.

For suggestions regarding honoring a loved one's memory see pages 171-173.

The sun will not harm you by day,

nor the moon by night...

The Lord will watch over

your coming and going

both now and forevermore.

Psalm 121: 6,8

My Letter

_____,

_____

_____

_____

_____

_____

_____

_____

_____

_____

_____

_____

_____

_____

_____

_____

_____

Believe

There is no mountain so high
You cannot climb it.
There is no river so wide
You cannot cross it.
There is no flower so small
You cannot touch it.
There is no music so soft
You cannot hear it.
There is no love so lost
You cannot find it...

Edna Louise

Memories are the key not to the past,

but to the future.

The experiences of our lives,

when we let God use them,

become the mysterious and perfect

preparation for the work

He will give us to do.

Corrie Ten Boom

In Remembrance

Tragedy and loss create enormous disruption. The world as you knew it has changed and those changes require that you in turn adjust to a "new normal." Changing your perception and behavior and moving in a new direction is not easy. In fact, it's probably the most difficult thing you'll ever do. For some, the mere thought of letting go causes great anxiety because they see it as a form of disloyalty. Occasionally someone will say to me, "But, if I let go it's like he never existed." I'm quick to reassure them that letting go doesn't mean dismissing the person from their life. Letting go means releasing the sorrow but cherishing the memories and recalling the joy that each one brought to the relationship.

Setting up a memorial can be a way of holding your special memories close to you and at the same time sharing them with others. There are no set rules for erecting a memorial. However, before you decide on a specific project, spend some time considering what would summarize the person's life in a loving and meaningful way. Gather mementos and memorabilia and look through them. Ask friends and family for input.

You may not be ready for months or perhaps years to consider a memorial. However, when you're ready, the following pages contain suggestions to help you get started.

God gave us memories

that we might have roses in December.

James M. Barrie

Memorial Garden

It can be a simple flowerbed or an elaborate garden that includes a fountain and/ or a pond. Be sure to include flowers and/or plants that had special significance to the person you're honoring.

Memory Book

Put together a collection of memorabilia that was meaningful to the person. It can include awards, pictures, newspaper clippings, art, etc.

Video

Encourage others to contribute pictures going back as far as possible. Include dates and captions and add his/her favorite music. Keep it cheerful and light-hearted.

Website

Write about the influence the person had in your life and in the lives of others. Include accomplishments at work and in the community and any volunteer work or charitable organizations they were involved with. Include pictures, stories, testimonials from friends, awards and accomplishments, etc.

He [God] is nearer to us
than we are to ourselves

A.W. Tozer

Donate

Make a contribution to his/her favorite charity or foundation in their name. Ask if the foundation will allow a plaque to be hung in their honor.

Volunteer

Consider spending two or three hours a week volunteering at their favorite charitable organization or one that they were associated with during their lifetime.

Scholarship

Consider setting up a new foundation that will help at-risk youth in the following ways: achieve their potential, acquire a college education, receive counseling and mentoring, etc.

Mentor

Seek out someone who is grieving due to loss and support and encourage them as a tribute to your loved one.

Keep in mind that while it's important for you to give yourself permission to grieve and mourn, it's equally important for you give yourself permission to accept healing and move forward with hope and purpose.

Part 2:

Life Regained

...for the Lord will be
your everlasting light,
and the days of your mourning
shall be ended.

Isaiah 60:20

Therefore, since we are surrounded
by such a great cloud of witnesses,
let us throw off everything that hinders
and the sin that so easily entangles,
and let us run with perseverance
the race marked out for us.

Hebrews 12:1

Introduction

One of the most common symptoms of grieving is depression. It's not unusual to experience sadness again and again as you progress through your healing journey. This may cause you to wonder if you're sliding backward rather than moving forward. However, you must not allow times of regression to discourage you. See them instead as evidence that you <u>are</u> healing but need to do more work at that particular stage.

Feelings of depression are especially common during holidays and other days that hold special significance, such as anniversaries and birthdays. Knowing ahead of time what to expect and preparing yourself for the possibility that you'll experience a resurgence of emotions will help minimize the impact. (See pages 205-211 for helpful suggestions.)

As stated previously, healing requires that you accept your loss, choose to let go and move forward in a new direction. Surrounding yourself with people who are understanding and supportive reminds you that you're not alone. Attending grief recovery support groups or workshops allows you to connect with others who are experiencing similar emotions and can provide insight and encouragement. Involvement in the community or in a project geared toward helping others can serve to take your attention away from yourself and your pain and give you a broader perspective. Several studies support the premise that helping others,

In the midst of difficulty
lies opportunity.

Albert Einstein

even if it means pushing yourself to do it, benefits the giver as much as it does the recipient.

As you continue healing you'll experience a lessening of grief and in time the memories associated with the severed relationship will be less painful. As you emerge whole and healed, your life may take an entirely different path—one that you may not have considered if it wasn't for the loss. In my case, it led to writing books and conducting "Healing From Loss" workshops.

Growing and learning from your experience and the demands that were placed upon you will enable you to understand and empathize with others who may be facing a similar loss and need your help. Pray for wisdom and guidance as you move forward.

If you can't fly then run.

If you can't run then walk.

If you can't walk then crawl.

But whatever you do,

You have to keep moving forward.

Martin Luther King Jr.

Looking Ahead

Now that you've spent a considerable amount of time working through a crisis in your life, you've gained insight and developed new skills. These skills will enable you to deal with any resurgence of emotions connected to your present loss and enable you to deal with new ones when they occur. Bit by bit you've peeled away the layers that were creating a barrier between you and your future and you're now ready to move forward.

Although the loss was not something you chose, you've learned and grown from the experience. As a result, you're better equipped to face the uncertainties of life and embrace every moment with grace and humility, forged with strength and courage. You're now free to welcome the blessings and meet the challenges that life offers without fear or excuses.

Life with all its challenges and joys, its peak moments as well as the ordinary and mundane, is a privilege and a gift from God. And when we consider all the possibilities that come our way, from the miniscule to the majestic, life is both— humbling and awesome.

Readers have shared with me that working through the various stages of healing and setting future goals was a huge step forward. My prayer is that your life will acquire new meaning as well as deep gratitude as you move toward the future that God has for you.

Reflect upon your present blessings,

of which every man has many—

not on your past misfortunes,

of which all men have some.

Charles Dickens

Living in the Present

You've lived though various experiences (good and bad) and will undoubtedly live through many more but each one will be experienced in the *present*, for the simple reason that the exact moment that you're living in—is the only moment that truly exists in this lifetime.

Living in the present means being mindful of what's taking place around you and being conscious of your feelings, attitudes and actions as they occur. Choosing to focus on the present is a decision to disallow worries or concerns about the past or the future to impinge upon the immediate moment. To be fully in the present, you must attend to what your sense of touch, smell, sight, hearing and taste are telling you and allow your mind and body to absorb the experience. It means accepting every situation as part of your reality whether it brings joy or sorrow or leads you in an entirely new direction.

In essence, living in the present means savoring each and every moment to its fullest with childlike faith and freedom, while trusting God to provide for your needs now and in the future.

The following pages will help you to connect with the present and evaluate your reactions.

Therefore I live for today —

certain of finding at sunrise

guidance and strength for the way.

power for each moment of weakness,

hope for each moment of pain,

comfort for every sorrow,

sunshine and joy after rain.

Billy Graham

What is happening around me right now?

_____

_____

_____

_____

_____

_____

_____

_____

_____

_____

_____

_____

How am I feeling?

_____

_____

_____

_____

_____

_____

_____

_____

_____

_____

_____

_____

_____

_____

Remember that you are needed.

There is at least one important work

to be done that will never be done

unless you do it.

Charles Allen

Discovering My Passion

Passion is a part of everyday life and encompasses the entire span of human existence, from birth to death. It can be found in the most ordinary and sometimes unlikely places—the stillness of a moonlit night, the shattering of silence by a screeching owl seeking its prey, the laughter of children as they turn cartwheels, fragile snow flakes hanging in the air before landing gently on your open palm, the smell of damp earth after a rainfall, the fervor of a mother intent on foraging for food in a war-torn country.

+ Passion is looking at ordinary life and finding the beauty, uniqueness and sometimes sadness contained within and allowing yourself to experience the feelings that it evokes in you.

+ Passion is reaching heavenward with one hand and with the other helping your neighbor.

+ Passion is living your life fully—with no explanations and no excuses.

The following pages will help you discover your passion and assist you in identifying your gifts and purpose in life.

May the God of hope

fill you with all joy and peace.

As you trust in him,

so that you may overflow with hope

by the power of the Holy Spirit.

Romans 15:13

How am I reacting to my feelings?

_____

_____

_____

_____

_____

_____

_____

What are my senses telling me right now?

Hearing:_____

_____

_____

Smelling:_____

_____

_____

Seeing: _____

_____

_____

Touching:_____

_____

_____

Tasting:_____

_____

_____

God has a great race for you to run.

Under His care,

you'll go where you've never been

and serve in ways

that you've never dreamed.

–Max Lucado

I get excited when I... *(listen to music, watch or play sports, garden, travel, teach, etc.)*

_____

_____

_____

_____

_____

_____

_____

_____

_____

_____

_____

_____

Things that I do well are...

_____

_____

_____

_____

_____

_____

_____

_____

_____

_____

_____

_____

_____

_____

Whatever your hand
finds to do,
do it with all your might...

Ecclesiastes 9:10

Things that other people say I do well are…

_____
_____
_____
_____
_____
_____
_____
_____
_____

Who do I enjoy being with?

_____
_____
_____
_____
_____
_____
_____

What activities do I enjoy doing?

_____
_____
_____
_____
_____
_____
_____
_____
_____

When one door closes

another door opens;

but we so often look so long

and so regretfully

upon the closed door,

that we do not see the ones

which open for us.

Alexander Graham Bell

What's preventing me from doing the activities I enjoy?

_____

_____

_____

_____

_____

_____

_____

_____

_____

_____

_____

_____

_____

_____

What can I do to overcome those obstacles?

_____

_____

_____

_____

_____

_____

_____

_____

_____

_____

_____

_____

_____

_____

"For I know the plans I have for you,"

declares the Lord,

"plans to prosper you and not to harm you,

plans to give you hope and a future."

Jeremiah 29:11

Planning For My Future

Many of the obstacles that were preventing you from making progress have been dealt with. Now it's time to look ahead and, with your newfound freedom, begin planning your future.

Writing down your goals will help solidify your commitment, give you a concrete plan and help you stay motivated. Use the information you entered in the section titled *Discovering My Passion* to start planning. Make any adjustments that you feel are necessary. Next, write down your goals for five and ten years from now. With those goals in mind, write down smaller ones that will lead you toward your desired results. Place the list in an area that's highly visible and easily accessible. If you stray from your goals, return to them as soon as possible. Rewrite them if necessary.

Be flexible and make any changes that you feel are important and will enable you to stay motivated. Reward yourself when you've made significant headway. Reaching long-range goals may take longer than you expected. However, staying motivated and working at a steady pace is more important than adhering to a strict timeline.

The following pages will help you plan your future and work toward achieving it— one step at a time.

The future belongs to those
who believe in the beauty
of their dreams.

Eleanor Roosevelt

Something that I've never done but would like to do is...

_____
_____
_____
_____
_____
_____
_____
_____
_____
_____
_____

My life would be more interesting and fulfilling if I did the following...

_____
_____
_____
_____
_____
_____
_____
_____
_____
_____
_____
_____
_____
_____

What has happened is not nearly
as important as what can happen.
Look to the possibilities of your future
for direction, forsaking the
burdensome limitations of your past.

Keith D. Harrell

What do I want to be doing five years from now?

_____
_____
_____
_____
_____
_____
_____
_____
_____
_____
_____
_____
_____
_____
_____
_____

What do I want to be doing ten years from now?

_____
_____
_____
_____
_____
_____
_____
_____
_____
_____
_____
_____
_____
_____
_____
_____

Set a goal,

write it down,

and release the outcome.

Small steps

make a big difference.

Cheryl Richardson

What do I need to do in order to get started? *(research the activity, write a detailed plan, enroll in a class, etc.)*

_____
_____
_____
_____
_____
_____
_____
_____
_____
_____
_____
_____
_____

What smaller goals can I set so that reaching my long-range goal is easier? *(Think of rungs on a ladder.)*

_____
_____
_____
_____
_____
_____
_____
_____
_____
_____
_____
_____
_____
_____

Do not be anxious about anything,

but in everything,

by prayer and petition,

with thanksgiving,

present your requests to God.

Philippians 4:6

Holidays and Special Events

Grief, and the emotions that accompany the loss of a loved one, is an agonizing experience. Seeing couples celebrating holidays and special events when your relationship has ended can seem like torture or at best, a dreaded event that makes you want to skip the celebration altogether. Below are a few suggestions to help minimize the stress and encourage you to heal.

Acknowledge Your Feelings

Give yourself permission to feel whatever it is you're feeling. Don't put on a happy face and assume you have to feel or behave a certain way. Tears can be a healthy release.

Take a Second Look

This may be a good time to examine your emotions and decide what you need to focus on and what you need to deal with in order to move forward.

Prayer and Praise

God knows your pain and is sustaining you through it. Write and post Bible verses that speak of His love and mercy such as: Jeremiah 29:11, Romans 8:18, Psalm 145:14. Praise lifts your heart and glorifies God. For inspiration read: Psalm 34:1, 1 Timothy 1:17, Psalm 63:3.

Be sure you put your feet

in the right place,

then stand firm.

Abraham Lincoln

Take Care of Yourself

Adequate rest and a healthy diet are important. Know your limit and don't push yourself to do more than you're able. Say "no" to activities that clutter your life. Go for a walk, read a book or listen to your favorite music. Eat foods that provide the nutrients your body needs.

Connect with Others

Being with friends and family is a reminder that you're not alone and encourages you to appreciate and nurture the relationships that you still have.

Ask for Help

Share your feelings. Getting help and support from others who understand your situation can make a big difference on your perception and attitude.

Seek Support

Consider joining a grief support group. Listening to the experiences of others and learning what has helped them can encourage and comfort you.

Make a Difference

Helping others can take the focus off yourself and your pain. Places such as nursing homes, homeless shelters and hospitals welcome volunteers. Mentoring a friend or family member who's struggling can be just as beneficial.

He gives power to the weak,

and to those who have no might

He increases strength.

Isaiah 40:29

Stop Comparing

Comparing yourself to others is a waste of time and can lead to frustration. Each person is unique and has special gifts and talents. Find yours and put them to use.

Rejoice for What You Have

Your loss is not the summation of your life. Consider the many things that you still have and enjoy them (faith, friends, family, job, home, health, etc.) Remember to smile and laugh often.

Know That You Will Survive

As painful as your loss is—you *will* survive. You'll get through the difficult times and when you do you'll be stronger and able to help others. If necessary re-read "My Journey Toward Healing Commitment" on page 75.

Your Choice

You don't have to enjoy or even participate in any festivity that's too much for you. However, if you choose to participate it's okay to enjoy yourself. Allow joy to happen naturally. The most wonderful gift you can give anyone you love, even someone who's no longer with you, is to live your life fully.

The life of one we love

is never lost...

its influence goes on

through all the lives

it ever touched.

Christopher Halloway

Consider Writing

This might be a good time to start keeping a journal. It can be a way of getting and staying in touch with your feelings. Write as much or as little as you want—even a sentence or two daily will help you stay focused and give you a different perspective.

While There's Life—There's Hope

Even though a previous relationship has ended, it doesn't mean that you'll never again experience peace and happiness. The key is to remain open and stay busy doing what you do best!

Whether you choose to participate in celebrating a holiday or special event or you decide to forego celebrating altogether, keep in mind that life is filled with new possibilities. Even changes that you didn't invite or want to happen can be opportunities for growing and exploring new avenues—ones that you might not otherwise have considered.

Part 3:

Life Reconnected

He that is thy friend indeed,

he will help thee in thy need:

if thou sorrow, he will weep;

If you wake, he cannot sleep;

thus of every grief in heart

he with thee doth bear a part.

Richard Barnfield

Therefore, encourage

one another

and build each other up...

1 Thessalonians 5:11

Introduction

The material contained in this section can be used as a resource for you to share with people who might not know how to help you and your family. It contains important insight and offers suggestions that they might not have considered.

However, the intended purpose of the material presented here is for you to help others who are grieving the same loss as yours. Due to the all-consuming characteristic of grief, it's easy to forget that others are also grieving. The list of people may include family, friends, or even coworkers. Their grief may or may not be as intense as yours, however it's just as real. Some of them, especially young children and teens, need direction, comfort and support and may be looking to you to provide it.

Lastly, this section contains valuable information that you can use to help others who are grieving their own loss apart from yours. Even though you're still grieving and may have a long way to go before you can claim complete healing, others have been observing you as you've gone through the experience. The courage and strength that you've shown, as well as your reliance on God, is a powerful testimony—one that you can use to support and encourage others.

The best in me

and the best in you

hailed each other

because they knew

that always and always

since life began,

our being friends

was part of God's plan.

George Webster Douglas

Connecting With Others

Loss is part of the human experience and can come from various sources. For a more detailed list see page 71.

Death	Finances
Divorce	Home
Employment	Pets
Health	Relationships
Miscarriage	Cherished Dream

Emotional reaction to loss can vary from minor to deeply intense—depending on your attachment to what has been lost. However, even anticipated situations such as changing jobs, relocating, or retirement can cause strong emotional reactions. When a friend or loved one is grieving, it's important to keep in mind that expressing grief is personal and individual. It not only varies from person to person but can vary from one day to the next for the same person.

Emotions tend to fluctuate even during times of relative calm. During a crisis emotions peak and plummet like a roller coaster that's out of control. Fortunately, God created humans with a desire for wellness. Even at the deepest point of grief, your spirit is seeking to heal and move past the anguish.

...comfort those in any trouble

with the comfort we ourselves

receive from God.

2 Corinthians 1:4

Grief and How You Can Help

The way in which people experience their grief depends on several factors in-cluding: personality, lived experiences, cultural background, religious beliefs, etc. Emotions many vary in magnitude and the manner in which they're expressed (crying, depression, anger, compulsive or reckless behavior, etc). Being some-one who's supportive and understanding without being judgmental is very im-portant. Even when you don't know exactly what to say to a grieving person, simply being present and available is comforting. A person's grief may be so deep that it causes a barrier between them and God. Offering to pray with them (even if it's only you who prays) can serve as a reminder that God cares and is "our refuge and strength, an ever-present help in trouble." (Psalm 46:1 NKJV)

It's also important that you validate their feelings and acknowledge their loss. One way that you can initiate conversation is by saying, "I heard about your loss. I'm truly sorry." Listening without judging and allowing them to express their feel-ings without censorship is crucial; so is expressing empathy without making their loss seem insignificant.

For additional suggestions on what to say and/or do when expressing sympathy see page 225.

As you grow older you will discover
that you have two hands.
One for helping yourself,
the other for helping others.

Audrey Hepburn

Other Ways of Helping

Oftentimes, reality sets in when the grieving person has to deal with life alone or in an entirely different way. Make a conscious effort to stay in touch with them by phone or email. You might also consider taking them out to lunch, going for a walk or doing other activities they enjoy. Offering to help with daily chores such as: grocery shopping, preparing a meal, childcare, driving them to appointments and housekeeping chores is another way to let them know you care.

Holidays and anniversaries can be particularly difficult after a loss and may cause the grieving person to experience intense feelings once again (see pages 205-211). Being sensitive and allowing them to express their sadness or other emotions will help them get through those rough days. Including them in holiday activities and/or celebrations, especially if they don't have family nearby, is also important. Sharing pleasant memories about the deceased can be a way of honoring their memory.

The important thing is to stay open and be sensitive as you make yourself available and regardless of how you choose to help, following through with your commitment is essential.

We make a living
by what we get,
But we make a life
by what we give.

Winston Churchill

Healing is a Process

Occasionally people will become impatient with themselves or others and want to rush the healing process. However, moving too quickly rather than allowing yourself the amount of time you need to grieve, can prolong healing and create additional chaos. Just as there is no right or wrong way to express grief, there is no time limit when grief should end. In fact, most people may experience a lessening of grief but never get over the loss completely. Although grieving may be experienced in stages, the stages do not necessarily follow a prescribed course. Reverting back to a previous stage or even skipping a stage altogether is not unusual.

Situational Versus Clinical Depression

It's important that you recognize if/when a person's grief is moving from situational depression to the more serious form—clinical depression. Situational depression is connected to a traumatic event. It encompasses many emotions and is interspersed with good and bad days.

Clinical depression on the other hand, is associated with feelings of deep despair and hopelessness. Some of the behaviors to watch out for include: disorientation, chemical abuse, deep sadness that seems to be getting worse, refusing proper hygiene care, death wish or talking about suicide. If someone you know is experiencing these symptoms you might want to suggest, in a non-confrontational way, that they consider going for counseling or joining a grief support group.

The friend who can be silent

with us in a moment

of despair or confusion,

who can stay with us in an hour

of grief and bereavement...

that is a friend who cares.

Henri Nouwen

Expressing Sympathy

What Not To Say (Clichés)

Be glad he/she lived a long life.

Everything happens for a reason.

Aren't you over him/her yet?

You can always have another child.

I know how you feel.

You have to be strong.

Time heals all wounds.

He's/She's in a better place.

You need to move on.

What To Say And/Or Do

I'm very sorry for your loss.

Please tell me how I can help you.

You & your family are in my thoughts & prayers.

Invite him/her to share.

Listen attentively.

Listen without judging.

Give him/her a hug. (Words aren't always necessary.)

We worry about what a child

will become tomorrow,

yet we forget that he is someone today.

Stacia Tauscher

Children and Bereavement

Children have a built-in tendency to sense when something is wrong. Letting them know (in age appropriate terms) when a close family member is seriously ill or has died, is much better than withholding information and speaking in hushed voices. Keeping children "in the dark" creates and air of mystery and impending doom. They have vivid imaginations and tend to put the worst possible interpretations on things they don't understand, especially when adults are being secretive. Talking to your kids about the situation will help them to better comprehend what's happening and lessen their anxiety.

Some points you need to keep in mind are:

- Keep the conversation brief and to the point (children have short attention spans).

- Use simple terminology that's age appropriate.

- Be honest but share only basic information.

- Reassure them that while the situation is sad, the world and their lives will continue.

- Ask them if they have any questions or concerns.

- Tell them they can come to you anytime they want to talk.

Children love, they laugh, they care.

Children, bless them, they know how to share.

Children try hard to be what you want...

So cherish the children these

Treasures from God, for without

Them the Earth would be nothing

But water and sod.

Dewey Nixon

Most cultures have established norms with respect to children being allowed to attend funeral services. Some cultures are reluctant, while others see it as a way to introduce them (while surrounded by family) to a reality which they will probably experience more than once in their lifetime.

My children were in their teens when their grandfather passed away. They attended the funeral services along with several cousins of various ages. Among those in attendance were many of Dad's friends who came with extended family members, including some three and four-year-olds. A particular case that stands out in my memory is the great grandfather who held his grandson (age 4) by the hand as he greeted the mourners. The elderly gentleman extended his hand to each of us and offered his condolences. The four-year-old followed his grandfather's example and extended his hand as he repeated the same phrase his grandparent had used.

The procedure, which was conducted in a natural and respectful manner, served not only to provide an example of appropriate behavior, it also implied that death is not something alien and cataclysmic but part of the human experience. The funeral service can also be a way for children to see the big picture and acquire a sense of closure they might not otherwise have.

While we try to teach

our children all about life,

Our children teach us

what life is all about.

Angela Schwindt

However, the decision whether to allow children to attend funeral services or not, is one that each parent needs to make with their own children in mind. Several factors that must be taken into consideration are: the child's age, maturity level, relationship to the deceased, current issues in the child's life, etc.

Regardless of your decision, the important thing to keep in mind is to provide constant reassurance of your love and willingness to talk as well as modeling an attitude of faith in God's mercy and protection. This will give them the security and foundation they need to help them heal and move forward in their own lives.

Children will not remember

you for the material things

you provided

But for the feeling

that you cherished them.

Richard L. Evans

Helping Children Adjust to Change

When dramatic changes or trauma occur in the lives of children, it's extremely important to reassure them of your love and protection. They also need to be told repeatedly that they are not responsible for your decision to end a relationship. If separation or divorce are involved, reassure them that they can continue to have a relationship with both of you, although the living arrangements have altered.

New situations require time to adjust. Expecting children to adapt quickly is unrealistic especially when several changes are involved, as is the case with relocating. You can minimize the stress by providing structure and maintaining a routine. Structure does not mean rigid adherence to rules; it means having a schedule they can depend on and preferably one they're already familiar with (meals, homework, playtime, bedtime, etc.). It's also important to adhere to the discipline and reward system that's already in place. This is not a time to bend the rules or allow children to get away with inappropriate behavior, however tempting that may be. Children, like adults, feel safe and secure when they know what to expect and have clear boundaries.

Kids need to share their feelings and know that they will not be punished for expressing them. When they share with you, listen carefully, acknowledge and validate what they're experiencing even if you don't fully understand. Two key factors to keep in mind when communicating with children are patience and under-

Jesus called the children to him and said,

"Let the little children come to me,

and do not hinder them,

for the kingdom of God

belongs to such as these."

Luke 18:16

standing. They don't always express themselves in ways that are clear and direct. If your child is having difficulty expressing him/herself, you might encourage conversation by saying. "You seem angry (sad, afraid). Can you tell me about it?" (See pages 53-55, 61.) Writing in a journal is another approach that older children can use to express themselves. For younger children who haven't yet learned to write, drawing pictures or using doll figures to role play is a good alternative.

Parents who are locked in ongoing conflict with each other can cause a lot of damage to their children. Resolve whatever conflict exists between you without involving the children. Resist the temptation to use them as pawns or place them in a position of having to choose between you.

Children vary in the way they adjust to major changes. Some experience few problems, others experience difficulty for the first few months, and still others seem to go from one problem to another without pausing. Some factors that may impact their adjustment include: age, level of maturity, amount of support, understanding of the situation, other trauma present, etc. (See pages 59-63.)

To console those who mourn...

to give them beauty for ashes,

the oil of joy for mourning,

the garment of praise

for the spirit of heaviness...

Isaiah 61:3

However, most kids will undergo a range of emotions as part of the adjustment process and may include the following:

Anger

It may be directed toward the parent(s) or caregivers whom they see as responsible for the change or it may be directed at siblings, pets, playmates or no one in particular. Their anger is usually expressed through misbehavior at home and/or school. They may also encourage their siblings to misbehave.

Anxiety and Fear

Both are common reactions to change and uncertainty and can show up in many ways including: excessive crying, nail biting, tics, bed-wetting, nightmares, clinging behavior, etc.

Depression

Feelings of sadness and brooding along with an attitude of hopelessness, lack of motivation and loss of interest is not unusual.

Regression

Many children experience feeling of helplessness, whining or return to behavior they had outgrown such as thumb sucking, nail biting, etc.

Please Note: Negative behaviors that escalates over time or are replaced by equally negative ones, are a strong indication that you need to seek professional advice without delay.

Teach Me to Pray

Though the road seems dark and the days seem long,

Teach me to pray and know right from wrong.

When confusion mounts and I feel a tear,

Help me to know you are forever near...

Most times I trust and believe in You,

Yet sometimes I doubt what is really true.

Help save me, dear Lord, from my disbelief,

From my wavering heart bring me relief...

Edna Louise

Some behaviors that require immediate attention include:

- Difficulty in sleeping

- Inability to concentrate

- Disruptive behavior at school

- Running away from home

- Drug or alcohol use

- Injuring themselves physically

- Injuring others and/or pets

- Eating disorders

- On-going anger or violent rages

- Withdrawal from family and friends

- Repeated school truancy

- Destroying property

It any of these behaviors are present, it's important that you discuss them with your child's health care provider, teacher(s), school counselor or a child therapist who can provide guidance and support in helping you deal with the issues.

Appendix

Prayer of St. Francis of Assisi

Lord, make me an instrument of Thy peace;

where there is hatred, let me sow love;

where there is injury, pardon;

where there is doubt, faith;

where there is despair, hope;

where there is darkness, light;

and where there is sadness, joy.

For it is in giving that we receive,

it is in pardoning that we are pardoned,

and it is in dying that we are born to eternal life.

Life Is

(Excerpt)

Life is an opportunity, benefit from it.

Life is beauty, admire it.

Life is a challenge, meet it.

Life is a promise, fulfill it.

Life is sorrow, overcome it.

Life is a tragedy, confront it.

Life is precious, do not destroy it.

Life is Life.

Mother Teresa

About the Author

Paulina Rael Jaramillo has a Master's degree in Rehabilitation Counseling from California State University, San Bernardino. She has worked with families and youth in various capacities, including crisis intervention and maintenance. Her hands-on experience has given her valuable insight into the damaging effects of trauma resulting from loss and the importance of dealing with negative emotions in order to move forward.

She began her writing career as a contributing writer for a regional newspaper and advanced to freelancing for Christian and secular magazines with national circulation. Her articles range from personal experience and current events to career and entertainment. She has contributed to eight inspirational books published by Starburst Publishers and Bethany House.

In 2009, she published her first book, *A Time to Heal: Grief Recovery Guide and Workbook,* and a year later wrote a follow-up book, *Life Interrupted: Grief Recovery Guide and Workbook* (revised 2015). Her fifth book (and third self-help) is titled, *Life Resumed: After a Catastrophic Event and Other Loss* (2020).

Paulina is currently conducting ongoing *Healing from Loss* workshops and shares her "grieving to healing story" on a variety of platforms.

Visit Paulina's website: **www.grief-recovery.org**
to download FREE Healing From Loss articles or to schedule a workshop.

Blog: https://paulinajaramillo.wordpress.com/

If my fire is not large
it is yet real,
and there maybe those
who can light their candle
at it's flame.

A.W. Tozer

Resource Guide

Websites

www.grief-recovery.org
Free articles addressing topics such as: Suicide, explaining death to children,
how to express sympathy, managing grief during the holidays and many more.

www.hospicenet.org
Assists patients and families facing life-threatening illness, loss, bereavement.

www.kidscamps.com
Summer camp directory, including special needs camps (e.g. bereavement).

www.kidsaid.com
A safe place for kids to help each other deal with grief and loss.

www.helpguide.org
Understand, prevent and resolve life's challenges. Relationship and health info.

www.aarp.org/family/lifeafterloss/
Tools to help with bereavement, checklists, wills/estate planning, memorials, etc.

www.griefnet.org
An internet community of persons dealing with grief, death, and major loss.

www.net-burst.net/
A faith-based website that comforts and inspires.

www.grieflossrecover.com/grief
Articles, poems, prayer requests.

www.divorcecare.com/healing/
Information to help with divorce recovery.

www.rileyguide.com
Online resource for anyone seeking employment or career-related information.

www.candlelightersnv.org
Provide support, education, hope and advocacy through programs and services
for children and adolescents with cancer and their families.

www.bereavedparentsusa.org/
Help bereaved parents, siblings and grandparents rebuild their lives.

www.picketfences.org/
A network of women helping women as they heal and make sense of the trauma
of a divorce and/or separation.

www.simplyhired.com/blog/
Job search website that includes advice and recruiting tips.

Now, may the Lord of peace

himself give you peace

at all times

in every way.

The Lord be with you all.

2 Thessalonians 3:16

Publications

A Grief Observed by C. S. Lewis (Paperback) Publisher: HarperOne; 1 edition (February 6, 2001).

What's Heaven by Maria Shriver (Hardcover) Publisher: Golden Books Adult Publishing (October 30, 2007).

When Bad Things Happen to Good People by Harold S. Kushner (Paperback) Publisher: Anchor (August 24, 2004).

The Grieving Garden: Living with the Death of a Child by Suzanne Redfern and Susan K. (Paperback) Publisher: Gilbert Hampton Roads Pub. Co. (April 4, 2008).

A Mother Loss Workbook: Healing Exercises for Daughters by Diane Hambrook (Paperback) Publisher: Harper Paperbacks; 1st edition (October 7, 1997).

Straight Talk about Death for Teenagers: How to Cope with Losing Someone You Love by Earl A. Grollman (Paperback) Publisher: Beacon Press; 1 edition (April 1, 1993).

Rescuing Sprite: A Dog Lover's Story of Joy and Anguish by Mark R. Levin (Hardcover) Publisher: Pocket Books; 1 edition (November 6, 2007).

Moving Forward After Divorce: Practical Steps to Healing Your Hurts, Finding Fresh Perspective, Managing Your New Life by David Frisbie and Lisa Frisbie (Paperback) Publisher: Harvest House Publishers; 1 edition (August 1, 2006).

Fired, Laid Off, Out of a Job: A Manual for Understanding, Coping, Surviving by Byron K. Simerson and Michael D. McCormick (Hardcover) Publisher: Praeger Publishers (August 30, 2003).

5 Necessary Skills To Keep Your Career On Track by Richard S. Pearson (Paperback) Publisher: Outskirts Press (May 22, 2009).

Two Homes by Claire Masurel, Publisher: Candlewick; Reprint edition (July 14, 2003)

Making Divorce Easier on Your Child by Nicholas Long and Rex L. Forehand, Publisher: McGraw-Hill; 1st edition (March 6, 2002)

Works Cited

"Helping Your Child Cope with a Disaster". http://www.CDC.gov/ Centers for Disease Control and Prevention. 2020.

"Lets Talk About It: For Parents and Caregivers". https://www.mentalhealth.gov/. US. Department of Health and Human Services. 2019.

"About Child Trauma". www.http://www.nctsn.org/ The National Child Traumatic Stress Network. 2020.

The Lord is my rock,

my fortress and my deliverer...

Psalm 18:2